Sports Are the Best!

SOCCER IS THE BEST!

by Daniel Nunn

PEBBLE
a capstone imprint

Pebble is published by Capstone,
1710 Roe Crest Drive, North Mankato, Minnesota 56003
capstonepub.com

Library of Congress Cataloging-in-Publication Data is available on the Library of Congress website.

ISBN: 9798875256318 (hardcover)
ISBN: 9798875256264 (paperback)
ISBN: 9798875256271 (ebook pdf)

Summary: Easy-to-read text and bright photographs describe the rules, positions, skills, stars, and more of soccer. A short quiz at the end of the book lets the reader test what they've learned.

Editorial Credits
Editor: Erika L. Shores; Designer: Hilary Wacholz; Media Researcher: Rebekah Hubstenberger; Production Specialist: Tori Abraham

Image Credits
Getty Images: Al Bello, 28, Alex Pantling, 21, Alexander Hassenstein, 8, Alistair Berg, 12, Brendon Thorne, 11, Dan Mullan, 7, Dean Mouhtaropoulos, 27, Drazen_, cover (left), 20, FatCamera, 24, golero, 18, Jamie Squire, 9, Lorado, 17, Matt McNulty, 23, Nazar Abbas Photography, 13, Photosomnia, 5, Tim Warner, 29, Yasser Bakhsh, 25; Shutterstock: Amparo Garcia, cover (right), cdrin, 4, Fotokostic, 26, halwani wani (soccer net), throughout, Paolo Bona, 15, Pro.Sto, cover (middle), Ringo Chiu, 6, sirtravelalot, 19, Volodymyr Krasyuk (soccer ball), back cover, spine, and throughout

Printed and bound in China. 006459

Table of Contents

Words in **bold** are in the glossary.

Super Soccer

Soccer is the most popular sport in the world. In most countries, it is called football. Around the world, many people get together to play soccer.

Many more people watch their favorite teams at soccer **stadiums**. Others watch games at home on TV along with millions of other fans. But just why is soccer so popular?

Star Players and Top Teams

Soccer is a game full of star players. Many top players play for lots of clubs during their careers. They may also play for their national teams.

Sophia Smith

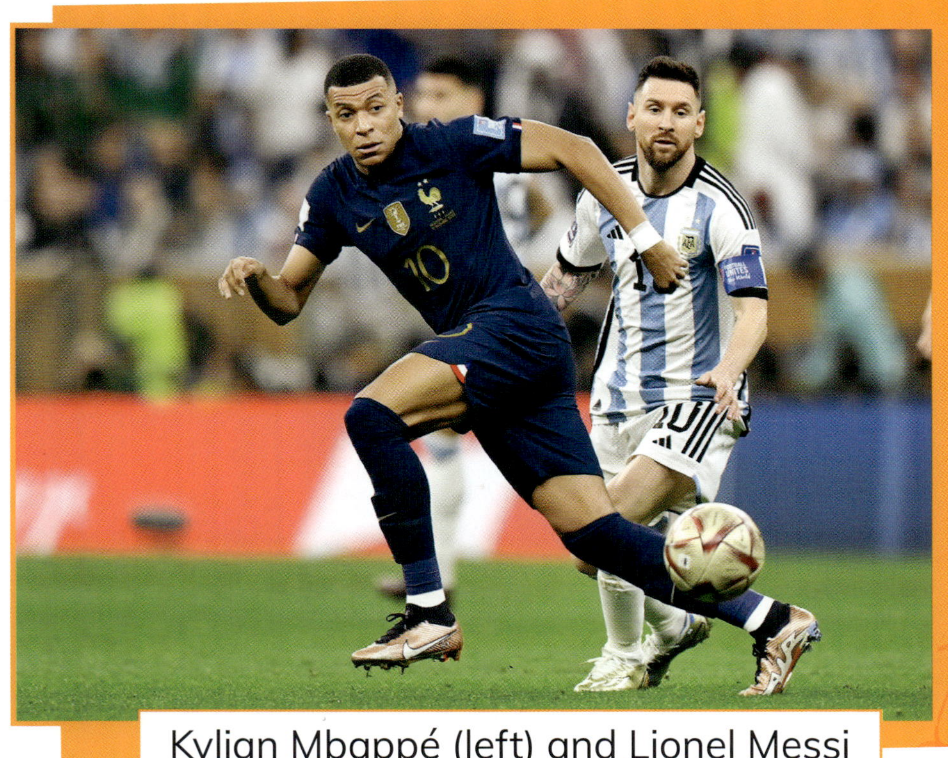

Kylian Mbappé (left) and Lionel Messi

The world's most famous women's players include the United States' Sophia Smith and England's Lauren James. Two of the top men's players are France's Kylian Mbappé and Argentina's Lionel Messi. But all fans have their favorites. Who are yours?

Soccer is also a game of star teams. Popular teams are Manchester City from England, Real Madrid from Spain, and Bayern Munich from Germany. In the United States, top men's teams include D.C. United and LA Galaxy. Top women's teams include the Orlando Pride and Washington Spirit.

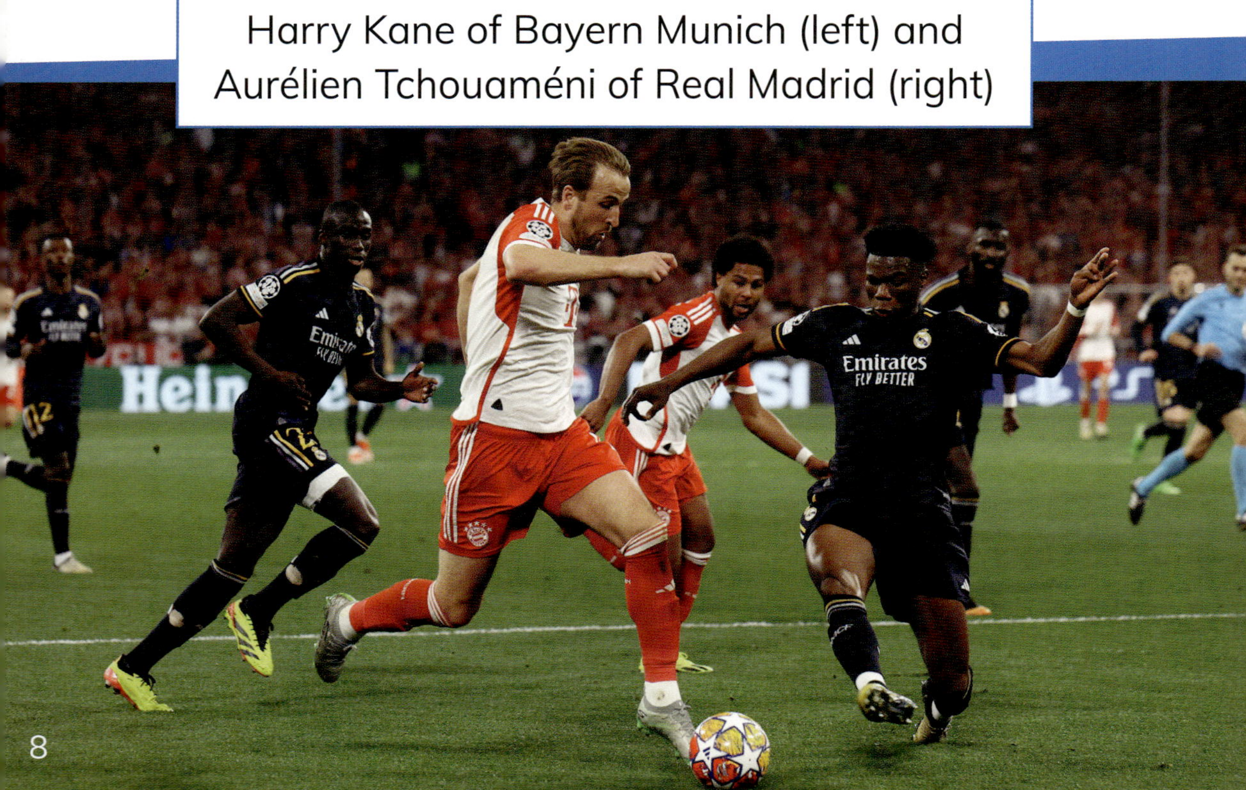

Harry Kane of Bayern Munich (left) and Aurélien Tchouaméni of Real Madrid (right)

But soccer isn't just about big teams! Even many small towns or schools have their own teams.

Marta (right) in action for the Orlando Pride.

In soccer, there are exciting competitions. In league competitions, all the teams play against each other to earn points. The team with the most points at the end wins.

Cup competitions are knockout competitions. Usually only the winner of a match goes on to the next round. In the World Cup, teams represent different countries. Argentina won the 2022 Men's World Cup. Spain won the 2023 Women's World Cup.

Spain (in red) and England (in blue) competed in the 2023 Women's World Cup final match.

What Do You Need to Play Soccer?

You don't need a lot of equipment to play soccer. All you really need is a ball. You can make **goalposts** out of anything.

If you are playing on a soccer team, you will need a pair of shin guards and soccer cleats. Cleats have studs on the bottom to stop you from slipping. You may also need a team uniform of a jersey, shorts, and socks.

You will also need somewhere to play. Most soccer teams play on a grass field called a pitch. The pitch has markings to show where to kick off, where to take **penalty kicks**, and more. There are goalposts at each end of the pitch.

A soccer match may also have a referee. The referee is an adult who makes sure that everyone is following the rules.

Joma
7

The Rules of Soccer

The main rule of soccer is easy to understand. You just need to score more goals than the other team! Easy!

The other team will try to stop you. They try to take the ball from you when you are running with it at your feet. They can also intercept **passes** to get the ball. Then it is their turn to try to score. It is your turn to try to stop them.

11

If you accidentally kick a player instead of the ball this is a foul. The referee can award a **free kick** or a penalty kick. If you are awarded a penalty kick, only the goalkeeper can stop you from scoring!

If a foul is dangerous and could have hurt the other player, the referee might show a card. A yellow card is a warning. A red card means the player has to leave the field. Their game is over.

Soccer Positions

Soccer players have different jobs. A goalkeeper's job is to protect the goal. They must stop the other team from scoring. They may even dive to block the ball with their hands.

Bradley Barcola of Paris Saint-Germain (left) and Ronald Araújo of FC Barcelona (center)

Defenders also try to stop the other team from scoring. It is their job to try to get the ball away from an **attacking** player. Then they pass it up the field toward the other team's goal.

A striker's job is to score goals. Strikers must be fast and good at avoiding the other team's defenders. They have to be able to kick the ball accurately to reach the goal.

Midfielders work in the middle of the pitch. Sometimes midfielders play in **defense** to try to stop the other team from scoring. Other times they will try to move the ball forward. Some midfielders also score lots of goals.

Khadija Shaw (in blue) of Manchester City and Sophie Baggaley (in red) of Brighton & Hove Albion

Soccer Skills

A good team has players with lots of different skills. Dribbling is when a player runs with the ball at their feet. You need to be good at controlling the ball. Otherwise, the other team might take it from you!

Jude Bellingham passes the ball for Real Madrid.

Passing is when you kick the ball to a teammate. You can pass it up the field or to a player who might score. You need to be accurate to make sure it goes to the right person.

You also need to be accurate to **shoot** at the goal. Some shots can be from a distance. You need to kick the ball hard but still be on target. Other shots can be from close range.

Tackling is when you try to get the ball away from another player with your feet. You need to be able to time your challenge just right! If you get it wrong, you might kick the player instead. Then the referee might award a free kick or a penalty kick! Oh no!

Josip Šutalo of Ajax tackles Rafa of Beşiktaş.

Is Soccer the Best?

Now you know all about soccer. It is a great game to enjoy with your friends—whether you are playing on a team or watching it as a fan.

Soccer is exciting to play and watch. It is easy to understand the rules. Lots of different skills go into making a great soccer team.

But is soccer the best sport? Millions of fans around the world think that it is!

Test Your Soccer Knowledge

Now that you've read this book, are you a soccer expert? Take this quiz to find out! If you don't know the answer, read the book again and you might be able to find it.

1. Can you name a famous player who plays for France? Is it:

    a. Lionel Messi

    b. Kylian Mbappé

    c. Lauren James

2. Which team won the Women's World Cup in 2023?

    a. United States

    b. England

    c. Spain

3. What does a red card mean?

    a. It's time for a snack break!

    b. The player needs to leave the field.

    c. The referee can't find their blue card.

Glossary

attacking (uh-TAK-ing)—moving toward the other team's goal

defense (DEE-fens)—the members of a team whose job it is to stop the other team from scoring

free kick (FREE KIK)—when a team is allowed to kick the ball while the opposing players are kept at a distance, usually after a foul has been committed

goalpost (GOHL-post)—a post marking one side of the goal

pass (PASS)—when a player kicks the ball to another player on the same team

penalty kick (PEN-uhl-tee KIK)—a kick awarded by the referee after a foul in the penalty area near the goal; only the other team's goalkeeper can try to stop the ball from going into the goal

shoot (SHOOT)—to try to kick the ball into the goal

stadium (STAY-dee-um)—a large building around a soccer pitch where professional soccer matches are played

Index

About the Author

Daniel Nunn is the author of dozens of nonfiction books for young readers. He is a huge soccer fan and enjoys going to both men's and women's soccer games with his children. His favorite team is Manchester City who play in England's Premier League.